It's easy to have a WORM to stay

Advisory Editor

Caroline O'Hagan R.A.N.A.

Illustrations by

Judith Allan

CHATTO & WINDUS · LONDON

An earthworm is a soft, crawly animal that lives under the ground and, if you would like to have a worm to stay, it is easy to catch one. Some kinds of worm make a cast, a little round squiggle of earth on the ground. If you see a worm-cast you know there has been a worm burrowing away underground.

You can dig in the earth almost anywhere that the soil is cool and moist and find an earthworm.

Before you look for your worm, you should make a special place for it to stay in while it visits you. Get two sheets of perspex or glass and three pieces of wood and make a tall, narrow box that you can see into. You can use a big jar, but you will be able to see more if your worm's box is tall and narrow.

Now fill up the box with layers of different coloured things like sand, earth, bone-meal, peat or compost. Most important of all is a layer of earth with plenty of leafmould in it, because this is what your worm eats.

Always keep your worm's box cool and moist — but don't make it too wet or your worm might drown.

Put your worm on top of its new home and have a good look at it. You will see that worms have no legs, feet or bones. If you wait for a minute or two you will see it begin to burrow.

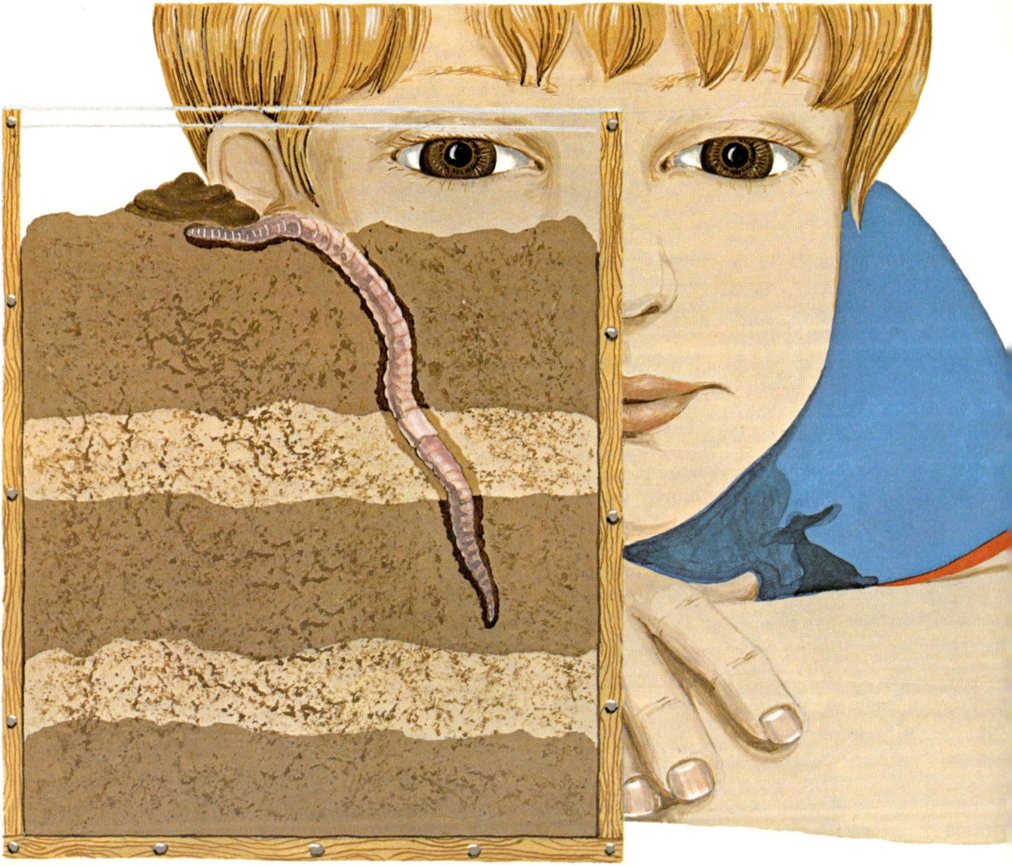

As your worm tunnels down it sucks the earth in, digests what it needs and leaves the rest behind. The earth it leaves behind is a worm-cast.

You can watch the patterns your worm makes as it moves through the different coloured layers of soil.

You can see why worms are so important. They break up big lumps of earth into smaller ones and spread goodness through the soil. The little tunnels they make let air in. Without worms, plants would not be able to grow so well.

Take your worm gently out of its place and put it on a piece of newspaper so you can watch closely how it moves. How does it move? It has hundreds of tiny hairs on its body which help it grip the soil. It stretches its body in the direction it wants to move, contracts, and then stretches out again. You will see that as it squirms along it seems to make its body fatter and thinner.

5p

When you put your worm back in its box, try giving it a little piece of leaf.

You may find that it uses the leaf to block up the top of its burrow. If the worm were outdoors, where it usually lives, this would keep out the cold and draughts.

You should not have your worm to stay for more than two weeks as it will begin to miss the real earth.

When you put your worm back in the ground, dig a little hole for it and cover it over gently with loose soil. Otherwise a bird might catch it before it has a chance to burrow!

Published by
Chatto & Windus Ltd
40 William IV Street, London WC2N 4DF

Clarke, Irwin & Co Ltd, Toronto

Edited, designed and produced by
Culford Books Limited
135 Culford Road, London N1

Edited by John Goldsmith
Designed by Judith Allan

First published 1980

ISBN 0 7011 2500 4

Printed and bound in Great Britain by
Waterlow (Dunstable) Ltd.